Fisher-Price®

Little People®

TODDLER WORKBOOK

PAGES
Colors
Fun
TEAR OUT

Written by Lauri Posner, M.S. Ed.
Educational Consultant, Robyn Ulzheimer

Cover illustration by Pattie Silver-Thompson
Interior illustrations by Georgene Griffin

Modern Publishing
A Division of Unisystems, Inc.
New York, New York 10022
Printed in the U.S.A.

DEAR PARENTS,

The Fisher-Price® Little People® Toddler Workbooks are an educational way to introduce your child to basic concepts. Research shows that encouraging learning at home has an important influence on your child's future success in school.

Following are some suggestions to keep in mind when using this book:

• Read through the book once, without your child. Cut out the manipulatives on the back pages and have them available for your child to use with selected activities. Many of the manipulatives can also be used as flash cards to reinforce learning.
• Choose a time in the day when your child is alert and able to focus. Limit the amount of time that you use these activities. This should be fun, and not work, for your child.
• Have a selection of pencils and crayons nearby.
• Ask questions of your child to prompt more meaningful learning. For example, when working on the blue pages, ask your child to find blue objects in your home. Extend the activities beyond the books whenever possible. Ask your child to look for different colors in their own environment at other times during the day.

Most of all, have fun with the book and enjoy the time you spend with your child.

BLUE

Can you find a picture of something else that is blue?

YELLOW

Can you find a picture of something else that is yellow?

4

RED

Can you find a picture of something else that is red?

GREEN

Can you find a picture of something else that is green?

ORANGE

Can you find a picture of something else that is orange?

PURPLE

Can you find a picture of something else that is purple?

BROWN

Can you find a picture of something else that is brown?

BLACK

Can you find a picture of something else that is black?

PINK

Can you find a picture of something else that is pink?

WHITE

Can you find a picture of something else that is white?

Finding Colors

Can you draw red circles around the red fish?
Can you draw blue circles around the blue fish?

Can you draw yellow circles around the yellow birds?
Can you draw green circles around the green birds?

Matching Colors

Can you draw a line to match the foods that are the same color?

Time to Color

Can you color the ice cream cone brown?
Can you color the ice cream pink?

Can you color the school bus yellow?

Can you color the umbrella blue?

Can you color the basketball orange?

Can you color the grapes purple?

More Colors Fun

Here are additional activities you can do with your child to help him or her learn colors.

• Mix paints with your child. Combine red and yellow paint to make orange, blue and red paint to make purple, and yellow and blue paint to make green. Add food coloring to vanilla icing. Mix different colors and decorate cupcakes with your child.

• Make a book with your child, with one page for each color. Look through magazines together to find pictures in each color and glue them to the appropriate page.

• Make clean-up time fun by asking your child to pick up all of his or her blue toys, then all of the red toys. Continue until the room is clean.

• Have your child match the solid colors on the manipulatives with the color words on pages 3-12.

• Read your child the following poem. Then ask your child to look around and name the colors of different objects in the room. Encourage your child's imagination by asking him or her to think up different colors for objects.

COLORS

Shut your eyes
What do you see?
A pretty pink flower
And a yellow bee.

Open your eyes
What is it now?
A black and white zebra
And a big brown cow.

Shut your eyes
What do you see?
A red and blue parrot
Eating a green pea.

Open your eyes
Blink once or twice.
Is that a purple pig
Eating orange ice?

• Use the cards on pages 29-32 to play a sorting game. Ask your child to sort the animals by color. There are green animals, brown animals, red animals, and black and white animals. Then have your child try to name other animals that could go with each group.

Manipulatives

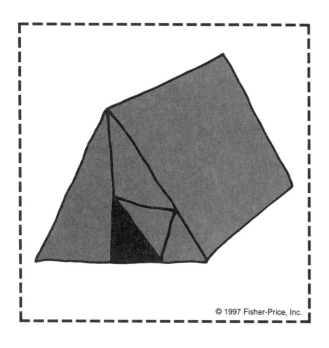

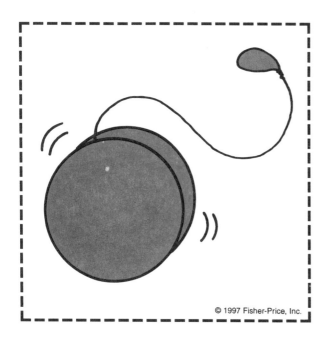

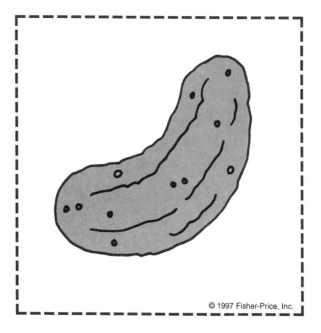

Cut out these cards for your child to use with selected activities.

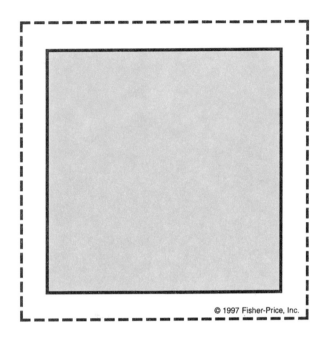

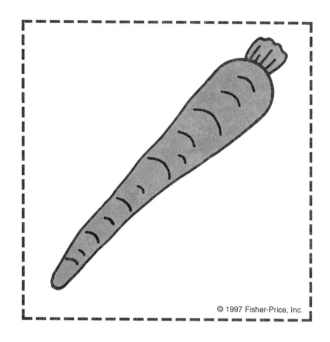

© 1997 Fisher-Price, Inc.

© 1997 Fisher-Price, Inc.

© 1997 Fisher-Price, Inc.

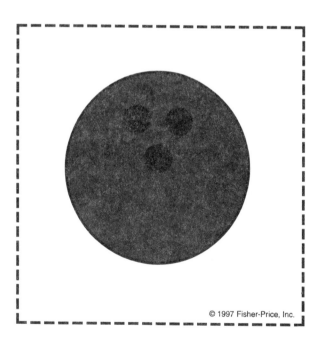

© 1997 Fisher-Price, Inc.

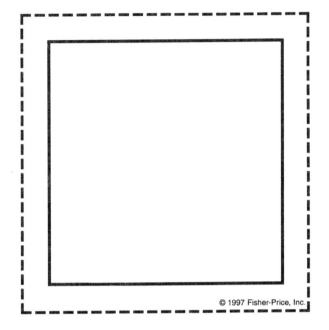

© 1997 Fisher-Price, Inc.

© 1997 Fisher-Price, Inc.

© 1997 Fisher-Price, Inc.

© 1997 Fisher-Price, Inc.

© 1997 Fisher-Price, Inc.

© 1997 Fisher-Price, Inc.

© 1997 Fisher-Price, Inc.

© 1997 Fisher-Price, Inc.

© 1997 Fisher-Price, Inc.

© 1997 Fisher-Price, Inc.